HELP
A Practical Guide
IN
to Everyday
DAILY
Blessings
LIVING

Pacific Press®
Publishing Association

Nampa, Idaho | Oshawa, Ontario, Canada
www.pacificpress.com

Cover design by Gerald Lee Monks
Cover design resources from iStockphoto.com
Interior design by Aaron Troia

Interior illustrations by
Robert Berran, artist, page 15, © Review and Herald® Publishing Association
Charles Zingaro, artist, page 30, © Pacific Press® Publishing Association
Russ Harlan, artist, page 57 © Review and Herald® Publishing Association

Additional copies of this book can be obtained by calling toll-free 1-800-765-6955 or by visiting http://www.adventistbookcenter.com.

Library of Congress Cataloging-in-Publication Data

  White, Ellen Gould Harmon, 1827-1915
  Help In Daily Living: a practical guide to everyday blessings / Ellen G. White
     p. cm
    Originally published 1964
    ISBN 978-0-8163-1884-1
    1. Christian life. I. Title
    BV4501.3. W46 2001
    248.4'86732—dc21
                     2001053099

February 2016

Contents

Preface

The four chapters which follow comprise the closing section of the popular and widely read *Ministry of Healing*. They have provided workable, down-to-earth, everyday guidance which has helped thousands to live successful Christian lives. To make these practical counsels available for convenient reading and rereading, they are now published in this compact form. Each chapter is a veritable mine of rich gems, worthy of recounting again and again as you face the practical realities of getting along with yourself, with others, and with God.

The author was a realistic Christian of rich experience with the Savior, and one ever alert to opportunities to render encouragement and help to those about her. Recognizing that true happiness is found only as we give, she viewed every Christian—layman, medical practitioner, and gospel laborer—as a "worker" interested in the welfare of others, and referred to such as "workers."

Carry this booklet with you. Read a portion as you have a free moment, and memorize some of the gems. Ponder the words and put them into practice. Life will become richer and more meaningful to you.

Board of Trustees of
THE ELLEN G. WHITE ESTATE

Everyday Living

There is an eloquence far more powerful than the eloquence of words in the quiet, consistent life of a pure, true Christian. What a man is has more influence than what he says.

The officers who were sent to Jesus came back with the report that never man spoke as He spoke. But the reason for this was that never man lived as He lived. Had His life been other than it was, He could not have spoken as He did. His words bore with them a convincing power, because they came from a heart pure and holy, full of love and sympathy, benevolence and truth.

It is our own character and experience that determine our influence upon others. In order to convince others of the power of Christ's grace, we must know its power in our own hearts and lives. The gospel we present for the saving of souls must be the gospel by which our own souls are saved. Only through a living faith in Christ as a personal Saviour is it possible to make our influence felt in a skeptical world. If we would draw sinners out of the swift-running current, our own feet must be firmly set upon the Rock, Christ Jesus.

The badge of Christianity is not an outward sign, not the wearing of a cross or a crown, but it is that which reveals the union of man with God. By the power of His grace manifested in the transformation of character the world is to be convinced that God has sent His Son as its Redeemer. No other influence that can surround the human soul has such power as the influence of an unselfish life. The strongest argument in favor of the gospel is a loving and lovable Christian.

The Discipline of Trial

To live such a life, to exert such an influence, costs at every step effort, self-sacrifice, discipline. It is because they do not understand this that many are so easily discouraged in the Christian life. Many who sincerely consecrate their lives to God's service are surprised and disappointed to find themselves, as never before, confronted by obstacles and beset by trials and per-plexities. They pray for Christlikeness of character, for a fitness for the Lord's work, and they are placed in circumstances that seem to call forth all the evil of their nature. Faults are revealed of which they did not even suspect the existence. Like Israel of old they question,

"If God is leading us, why do all these things come upon us?"

It is because God is leading them that these things come upon them. Trials and obstacles are the Lord's chosen methods of discipline and His appointed conditions of success. He who reads the hearts of men knows their characters better than they themselves know them. He sees that some have powers and susceptibilities which, rightly directed, might be used in the advancement of His work. In His providence He brings these persons into different positions and varied circumstances that they may discover in their character the defects which have been concealed from their own knowledge. He gives them opportunity to correct these defects and to fit themselves for His service. Often He permits the fires of affliction to assail them that they may be purified.

The fact that we are called upon to endure trial shows that the Lord Jesus sees in us something precious which He desires to develop. If He saw in us nothing whereby He might glorify His name, He would not spend time in refining us. He does not cast worthless stones into His furnace. It is valuable ore that He refines. The blacksmith puts the iron and steel into the fire that he may know what manner of metal they are. The Lord allows His chosen ones to be placed in the furnace of affliction to prove what temper they are of and whether they can be fashioned for His work.

The potter takes the clay and molds it according to his will. He kneads it and works it. He tears it apart and presses it together. He wets it and then dries it. He lets it lie for a while without touching it. When it is perfectly pliable, he continues the work of making of it a vessel. He forms it into shape and on the wheel trims and polishes it. He dries it in the sun and bakes it in the oven. Thus it becomes a vessel fit for use. So the great Master Worker desires to mold and fashion us. And as the clay is in the hands of the potter, so are we to be in His hands. We are not to try to do the work of the potter. Our part is to yield ourselves to be molded by the Master Worker.

"Beloved, think it not strange concerning the fiery trial which is to try you, as though some strange thing happened unto you: but rejoice, inasmuch as ye are partakers of Christ's sufferings; that, when His glory shall be revealed, ye may be glad also with exceeding joy." 1 Peter 4:12, 13.

In the full light of day, and in hearing of the music of other voices, the caged bird will not sing the song that his master seeks to teach him. He learns a snatch of this, a trill of that, but never a separate and entire melody. But the master covers the cage, and places it where the bird will listen to the one song he is to sing. In the dark, he tries and tries again to sing that song until it is learned, and he breaks forth in perfect melody. Then the bird is brought forth, and ever after he can sing that song in the light. Thus God deals with His children. He has a song to teach us, and when we have learned it amid the shadows of affliction we can sing it ever afterward.

God's Choice in Our Lifework

Many are dissatisfied with their lifework. It may be that their surroundings are uncongenial; their time is occupied with commonplace work, when they think themselves capable of higher responsibilities; often their efforts seem to them to be unappreciated or fruitless; their future is uncertain.

Let us remember that while the work we have to do may not be our choice, it is to be accepted as God's choice for us. Whether pleasing or unpleasing, we are to do the duty that lies nearest. "Whatsoever thy hand findeth to do, do it with thy might; for there is no work, nor device, nor knowledge, nor wisdom, in the grave, whither thou goest." Ecclesiastes 9:10.

If the Lord desires us to bear a message to Nineveh, it will not be as pleasing to Him for us to go to Joppa or to Capernaum. He has reasons for sending us to the place toward which our feet have been directed. At that very place there may be someone in need of the help we can give. He who sent Philip to the Ethiopian councilor, Peter to the Roman centurion, and the little Israelitish maiden to the help of Naaman, the Syrian captain, sends men and women and youth today as His representatives to those in need of divine help and guidance.

God's Plans the Best

Our plans are not always God's plans. He may see that it is best for us and for His cause to refuse our very best intentions, as He did in the case of David. But of one thing we may be assured, He will bless and use in the advancement of His cause those who sincerely devote themselves and all they have to His glory. If He sees it best not to grant their desires He will counterbalance the refusal by giving them tokens of His love and entrusting to them another service.

In His loving care and interest for us, often He who understands us better than we understand ourselves refuses to permit us selfishly to seek the gratification of our own ambition. He does not permit us to pass by the homely but sacred duties that lie next us. Often these duties afford the very training essential to prepare us for a higher work. Often our plans fail that God's plans for us may succeed.

We are never called upon to make a real sacrifice for God. Many things He asks us to yield to Him, but in doing this we are but giving up that which hinders us in the heavenward way. Even when called upon to surrender those things which in themselves are good, we may be sure that God is thus working out for us some higher good.

In the future life the mysteries that here have annoyed and disappointed us will be made plain. We shall see that our seemingly unanswered prayers and disappointed hopes have been among our greatest blessings.

We are to look upon every duty, however humble, as sacred because it is a part of God's service. Our daily prayer should be, "Lord, help me to do my best. Teach me how to do better work. Give me energy and cheerfulness. Help me to bring into my service the loving ministry of the Saviour."

A Lesson From the Life of Moses

Consider the experience of Moses. The education he received in Egypt as the king's grandson and the prospective heir to the throne was very thorough. Nothing was neglected that was calculated to make him a wise man, as the Egyptians understood wisdom. He received the highest civil and military training. He felt that he was fully prepared for the work of delivering Israel from bondage. But God judged otherwise. His providence appointed Moses forty years of training in the wilderness as a keeper of sheep.

The education that Moses had received in Egypt was a help to him in many respects; but the most valuable preparation for his lifework was that which he received while employed as a shepherd. Moses was naturally of an impetuous spirit. In Egypt a successful military leader and a favorite with the king and the nation, he had been accustomed to receiving praise and flattery. He had attracted the people to himself. He hoped to accomplish by his own powers the work of delivering Israel. Far different were the lessons he had to learn as God's representative. As he led his flocks through the wilds of the mountains and into the green pastures of the valleys, he learned faith and meekness, patience, humility, and self-forgetfulness. He learned to care for the weak, to nurse the sick, to seek after the straying, to bear with the unruly, to tend the lambs, and to nurture the old and the feeble.

In this work Moses was drawn nearer to the Chief Shepherd. He became closely united to the Holy One of Israel. No longer did he plan to do a great work. He sought to do faithfully as unto God the work committed to his charge. He recognized the presence of God in his surroundings. All nature spoke to him of the Unseen One. He knew God as a personal God, and, in meditating upon His character he grasped more and more fully the sense of His presence. He found refuge in the everlasting arms.

After this experience, Moses heard the call from heaven to exchange his shepherd's crook for the rod of authority; to leave his flock of sheep and take the leadership of Israel. The divine command found him self-distrustful, slow of speech, and timid. He was overwhelmed with a sense of his incapacity to be a mouthpiece for God. But he accepted the work, putting his

whole trust in the Lord. The greatness of his mission called into exercise the best powers of his mind. God blessed his ready obedience, and he became eloquent, hopeful, self-possessed, fitted for the greatest work ever given to man. Of him it is written: "There hath not arisen a prophet since in Israel like unto Moses, whom Jehovah knew face to face." Deuteronomy 34:10, A.R.V.

Let those who feel that their work is not appreciated, and who crave a position of greater responsibility, consider that "promotion cometh neither from the east, nor from the west, nor from the south. But God is the Judge: He putteth down one, and setteth up another." Psalm 75:6, 7. Every man has his place in the eternal plan of heaven. Whether we fill that place depends upon our own faithfulness in co-operating with God.

We need to beware of self-pity. Never indulge the feeling that you are not esteemed as you should be, that your efforts are not appreciated, that your work is too difficult. Let the memory of what Christ has endured for us silence every murmuring thought. We are treated better than was our Lord. "Seekest thou great things for thyself? seek them not." Jeremiah 45:5. The Lord has no place in His work for those who have a greater desire to win the crown than to bear the cross. He wants men who are more intent upon doing their duty than upon receiving their reward—men who are more solicitous for principle than for promotion.

Those who are humble, and who do their work as unto God, may not make so great a show as do those who are full of bustle and self-importance; but their work counts for more. Often those who make a great parade call attention to self, interposing between the people and God, and their work proves a failure. "Wisdom is the principal thing; therefore get wisdom: and with all thy getting get understanding. Exalt her, and she shall promote thee: she shall bring thee to honor, when thou dost embrace her." Proverbs 4:7, 8.

Because they have not the determination to take themselves in hand and to reform, many become stereotyped in a wrong course of action. But this need not be. They may cultivate their powers to do the very best kind of service, and then they will be always in demand. They will be valued for all that they are worth.

If any are qualified for a higher position, the Lord will lay the burden, not alone on them, but on those who have tested them, who know their worth, and who can understandingly urge them forward. It is those who perform faithfully their appointed work day by day, who in God's own time will hear His call, "Come up higher."

While the shepherds were watching their flocks on the hills of Bethlehem, angels from heaven visited them. So today while the humble worker for God is following his employment, angels of God stand by his side, listening to his words, noting the manner in which his work is done, to see if larger responsibilities may be entrusted to his hands.

True Greatness

Not by their wealth, their education, or their position does God estimate men. He estimates them by their purity of motive and their beauty of character. He looks to see how much of His Spirit they possess and how much of His likeness their life reveals. To be great in God's kingdom is to be as a little child in humility, in simplicity of faith, and in purity of love.

"Ye know," Christ said, "that the rulers of the Gentiles lord it over them, and their great ones exercise authority over them. Not so shall it be among you: but whosoever would become great among you shall be your minister." Matthew 20:25, 26, A.R.V.

Of all the gifts that heaven can bestow upon men, fellowship with Christ in His sufferings is the most weighty trust and the highest honor. Not Enoch, who was translated to heaven, not Elijah, who ascended in a chariot of fire, was greater or more honored than John the Baptist, who perished alone in the dungeon. "Unto you it is given in the behalf of Christ, not only to believe on Him, but also to suffer for His sake." Philippians 1:29.

Plans for the Future

Many are unable to make definite plans for the future. Their life is unsettled. They cannot discern the outcome of affairs, and this often fills them with anxiety and unrest. Let us remember that the life of God's children in this world is a pilgrim life. We have not wisdom to plan our own lives. It is not for us to shape our future. "By faith Abraham, when he was called to go out into a place which he should after receive for an inheritance, obeyed; and he went out, not knowing whither he went." Hebrews 11:8.

Christ in His life on earth made no plans for Himself. He accepted God's plans for Him, and day by day the Father unfolded His plans. So should we depend upon God, that our lives may be the simple outworking of His will. As we commit our ways to Him, He will direct our steps.

Too many, in planning for a brilliant future, make an utter failure. Let God plan for you. As a little child, trust to the guidance of Him who will "keep the feet of His saints." 1 Samuel 2:9. God never leads His children otherwise than they would choose to be led, if they could see the end from the beginning and discern the glory of the purpose which they are fulfilling as co-workers with Him.

Wages

When Christ called His disciples to follow Him, He offered them no flattering prospects in this life. He gave them no promise of gain or worldly honor, nor did they make any stipulation as to what they should receive. To Matthew as he sat at the receipt of custom, the Saviour said, "Follow Me. And he left all, rose up, and followed Him." Luke 5:27, 28. Matthew did not, before rendering service, wait to demand a certain salary equal to the amount received in his former occupation. Without question or hesitation he followed Jesus. It was enough for him that he was to be with the Saviour, that he might hear His words and unite with Him in His work.

So it was with the disciples previously called. When Jesus bade Peter and his companions follow Him, immediately they left their boats and nets. Some of these disciples had friends dependent on them for support; but when they received the Saviour's invitation they did not hesitate and inquire, "How shall I live and sustain my family?" They were obedient to the call; and when afterward Jesus asked them, "When I sent you without purse, and scrip, and shoes, lacked ye anything?" they could answer, "Nothing." Luke 22:35.

Today the Saviour calls us, as He called Matthew and John and Peter, to His work. If our hearts are touched by His love, the question of compensation will not be uppermost in our minds. We shall rejoice to be co-workers with Christ, and we shall not fear to trust His care. If we make God our strength we shall have clear perceptions of duty, unselfish aspirations; our life will be actuated by a noble purpose which will raise us above sordid motives.

God Will Provide

Many who profess to be Christ's followers have an anxious, troubled heart because they are afraid to trust themselves with God. They do not make a complete surrender to Him, for they shrink from the consequences that such a surrender may involve. Unless they do make this surrender they cannot find peace.

There are many whose hearts are aching under a load of care because they seek to reach the world's standard. They have chosen its service, accepted its perplexities, adopted its customs. Thus their character is marred and their life made a weariness. The continual worry is wearing out the life forces. Our Lord desires them to lay aside this yoke of bondage. He invites them to accept His yoke; He says, "My yoke is easy, and My burden is light." Worry is blind and cannot discern the future; but Jesus sees the end from the beginning. In every difficulty He has His way prepared to bring relief. "No good thing will He withhold from them that walk uprightly." Matthew 11:30; Psalm 84:11.

Our heavenly Father has a thousand ways to provide for us of which we know nothing. Those who accept the one principle of making the service of God supreme, will find perplexities vanish and a plain path before their feet.

The faithful discharge of today's duties is the best preparation for tomorrow's trials. Do not gather together all tomorrow's liabilities and cares and add them to the burden of today. "Sufficient unto the day is the evil thereof." Matthew 6:34.

Let us be hopeful and courageous. Despondency in God's service is sinful and unreasonable. He knows our every necessity. To the omnipotence of the King of kings our covenant-keeping God unites the gentleness and care of the tender shepherd. His power is absolute, and it is the pledge of the sure fulfillment of His promises to all who trust in Him. He has means for the removal of every difficulty, that those who serve Him and respect the means He employs may be sustained. His love is as far above all other love as the heavens are above the earth. He watches over His children with a love that is measureless and everlasting.

In the darkest days, when appearances seem most forbidding, have faith in God. He is working out His will, doing all things well in behalf of His people. The strength of those who love and serve Him will be renewed day by day.

He is able and willing to bestow upon His servants all the help they need. He will give them the wisdom which their varied necessities demand.

Said the tried apostle Paul: "He said unto me, My grace is sufficient for thee: for My strength is made perfect in weakness. Most gladly therefore will I rather glory in my infirmities, that the power of Christ may rest upon me. Therefore I take pleasure in infirmities, in reproaches, in necessities, in persecutions, in distresses for Christ's sake: for when I am weak, then am I strong." 2 Corinthians 12:9, 10.

Living With Others

Every association of life calls for the exercise of self-control, forbearance, and sympathy. We differ so widely in disposition, habits, education, that our ways of looking at things vary. We judge differently. Our understanding of truth, our ideas in regard to the conduct of life, are not in all respects the same. There are no two whose experience is alike in every particular. The trials of one are not the trials of another. The duties that one finds light are to another most difficult and perplexing.

So frail, so ignorant, so liable to misconception is human nature, that each should be careful in the estimate he places upon another. We little know the bearing of our acts upon the experience of others. What we do or say may seem to us of little moment, when, could our eyes be opened, we should see that upon it depended the most important results for good or for evil.

Consideration for Burden Bearers

Many have borne so few burdens, their hearts have known so little real anguish, they have felt so little perplexity and distress in behalf of others, that they cannot understand the work of the true burden bearer. No more capable are they of appreciating his burdens than is the child of understanding the care and toil of his burdened father. The child may wonder at his father's fears and perplexities. These appear needless to him. But when years of experience shall have been added to his life, when he himself comes to bear its burdens, he will look back upon his father's life and understand that which was once so incomprehensible. Bitter experience has given him knowledge.

The work of many a burden bearer is not understood, his labors are not appreciated, until death lays him low. When others take up the burdens he has laid down, and meet the difficulties he encountered, they can understand how his faith and courage were tested. Often then the mistakes they were so quick to censure are lost sight of. Experience teaches them sympathy. God permits men to be placed in positions of responsibility. When they err, He has power to correct or to remove them. We should be careful not to take into our hands the work of judging that belongs to God.

The conduct of David toward Saul has a lesson. By command of God, Saul had been anointed as king over

Israel. Because of his disobedience the Lord declared that the kingdom should be taken from him; and yet how tender and courteous and forbearing was the conduct of David toward him! In seeking the life of David, Saul came into the wilderness and, unattended, entered the very cave where David with his men of war lay hidden. "And the men of David said unto him, Behold the day of which the Lord said unto thee, . . . I will deliver thine enemy into thine hand, that thou mayest do to him as it shall seem good unto thee. . . . And he said unto his men, The Lord forbid that I should do this thing unto my master, the Lord's anointed, to stretch forth mine hand against him, seeing he is the anointed of the Lord." The Saviour bids us, "Judge not, that ye be not judged. For with what judgment ye judge, ye shall be judged: and with what measure ye mete, it shall be measured to you again." Remember that soon your life record will pass in review before God. Remember, too, that He has said, "Thou art inexcusable, O man, whosoever thou art that judgest: . . . for thou that judgest doest the same things." 1 Samuel 24:4-6; Matthew 7:1, 2; Romans 2:1.

Forbearance Under Wrong

We cannot afford to let our spirits chafe over any real or supposed wrong done to ourselves. Self is the enemy we most need to fear. No form of vice has a more baleful effect upon the character than has human passion not under the control of the Holy Spirit. No other victory we can gain will be so precious as the victory gained over self.

We should not allow our feelings to be easily wounded. We are to live, not to guard our feelings or our reputation, but to save souls. As we become interested in the salvation of souls we cease to mind the little differences that so often arise in our association with one another. Whatever others may think of us or do to us, it need not disturb our oneness with Christ, the fellowship of the Spirit. "What glory is it, if, when ye be buffeted for your faults, ye shall take it patiently? but if, when ye do well, and suffer for it, ye take it patiently, this is acceptable with God." 1 Peter 2:20.

Do not retaliate. So far as you can do so, remove all cause for misapprehension. Avoid the appearance of evil. Do all that lies in your power, without the sacrifice of principle, to conciliate others. "If thou bring thy gift to the altar, and there rememberest that thy brother hath aught against thee; leave there thy gift before the altar, and go thy way; first be reconciled to thy brother, and then come and offer thy gift." Matthew 5:23, 24.

If impatient words are spoken to you, never reply in the same spirit. Remember that "a soft answer turneth away wrath." Proverbs 15:1. And there is wonderful power in silence. Words spoken in reply to one who is angry sometimes serve only to exasperate. But anger met with silence, in a tender, forbearing spirit, quickly dies away.

Under a storm of stinging, faultfinding words, keep the mind stayed upon the Word of God. Let mind and heart be stored with God's promises. If you are ill-treated or wrongfully accused, instead of returning an angry answer, repeat to yourself the precious promises:

"Be not overcome of evil, but overcome evil with good." Romans 12:21.

"Commit thy way unto the Lord; trust also in Him; and He shall bring it to pass. And He shall bring forth thy righteousness as the light, and thy judgment as the noonday." Psalm 37:5, 6.

"There is nothing covered, that shall not be revealed; neither hid, that shall not be known." Luke 12:2.

"Thou hast caused men to ride over our heads; we went through fire and through water: but Thou broughtest us out into a wealthy place." Psalm 66:12.

We are prone to look to our fellow men for sympathy and uplifting, instead of looking to Jesus. In His mercy and faithfulness God often permits those in whom we place confidence to fail us, in order that we may learn the folly of trusting in man and making flesh our arm. Let us trust fully, humbly, unselfishly in God. He knows the sorrows that we feel to the depths of our being, but which we cannot express. When all things seem dark and unexplainable, remember the words of Christ, "What I do thou knowest not now; but thou shalt know hereafter." John 13:7.

Study the history of Joseph and of Daniel. The Lord

did not prevent the plottings of men who sought to do them harm; but He caused all these devices to work for good to His servants who amidst trial and conflict preserved their faith and loyalty.

So long as we are in the world, we shall meet with adverse influences. There will be provocations to test the temper; and it is by meeting these in a right spirit that the Christian graces are developed. If Christ dwells in us, we shall be patient, kind, and forbearing, cheerful amid frets and irritations. Day by day and year by year we shall conquer self, and grow into a noble heroism. This is our allotted task; but it cannot be accomplished without help from Jesus, resolute decision, unwavering purpose, continual watchfulness, and unceasing prayer. Each one has a personal battle to fight. Not even God can make our characters noble or our lives useful, unless we become co-workers with Him. Those who decline the struggle lose the strength and joy of victory.

Count God's Blessings, Not the Trials

We need not keep our own record of trials and difficulties, griefs, and sorrows. All these things are written in the books, and heaven will take care of them. While we are counting up the disagreeable things, many things that are pleasant to reflect upon are passing from memory, such as the merciful kindness of God surrounding us every moment and the love over which angels marvel,

that God gave His Son to die for us. If as workers for Christ you feel that you have had greater cares and trials than have fallen to the lot of others, remember that for you there is a peace unknown to those who shun these burdens. There is comfort and joy in the service of Christ. Let the world see that life with Him is no failure.

If you do not feel lighthearted and joyous, do not talk of your feelings. Cast no shadow upon the lives of others. A cold, sunless religion never draws souls to Christ. It drives them away from Him into the nets that Satan has spread for the feet of the straying. Instead of thinking of your discouragements, think of the power you can claim in Christ's name. Let your imagination take hold upon things unseen. Let your thoughts be directed to the evidences of the great love of God for you. Faith can endure trial, resist temptation, bear up under disappointment. Jesus lives as our Advocate. All is ours that His mediation secures.

Think you not that Christ values those who live wholly for Him? Think you not that He visits those who, like the beloved John in exile, are for His sake in hard and trying places? God will not suffer one of His truehearted workers to be left alone, to struggle against great odds and be overcome. He preserves as a precious jewel everyone whose life is hid with Christ in Him. Of every such one He says: "I . . . will make thee as a signet: for I have chosen thee." Haggai 2:23.

Then talk of the promises; talk of Jesus' willingness

to bless. He does not forget us for one brief moment. When, notwithstanding disagreeable circumstances, we rest confidingly in His love, and shut ourselves in with Him, the sense of His presence will inspire a deep, tranquil joy. Of Himself Christ said: "I do nothing of Myself; but as My Father hath taught Me, I speak these things. And He that sent Me is with Me: the Father hath not left Me alone; for I do always those things that please Him." John 8:28, 29.

The Father's presence encircled Christ, and nothing befell Him but that which infinite love permitted for the blessing of the world. Here was His source of comfort, and it is for us. He who is imbued with the Spirit of Christ abides in Christ. Whatever comes to him comes from the Saviour, who surrounds him with His presence. Nothing can touch him except by the Lord's permission. All our sufferings and sorrows, all our temptations and trials, all our sadness and griefs, all our persecutions and privations, in short, all things work together for our good. All experiences and circumstances are God's workmen whereby good is brought to us.

Speak No Evil

If we have a sense of the long-suffering of God toward us, we shall not be found judging or accusing others. When Christ was living on the earth, how surprised His associates would have been, if, after becoming acquainted with Him, they had heard Him speak one word of accusation, of fault-finding, or of impatience. Let us never forget that those who love Him are to represent Him in character.

"Be kindly affectioned one to another with brotherly love; in honor preferring one another." "Not rendering evil for evil, or railing for railing: but contrariwise blessing; knowing that ye are thereunto called, that ye should inherit a blessing." Romans 12:10; 1 Peter 3:9.

Courtesy

The Lord Jesus demands our acknowledgment of the rights of every man. Men's social rights, and their rights as Christians, are to be taken into consideration. All are to be treated with refinement and delicacy, as the sons and daughters of God.

Christianity will make a man a gentleman. Christ was courteous, even to His persecutors; and His true followers will manifest the same spirit. Look at Paul when brought before rulers. His speech before Agrippa is an illustration of true courtesy as well as persuasive eloquence. The gospel does not encourage the formal politeness current with the world, but the courtesy that springs from real kindness of heart.

The most careful cultivation of the outward proprieties of life is not sufficient to shut out all fretfulness, harsh judgment, and unbecoming speech. True refinement will never be revealed so long as self is considered as the supreme object. Love must dwell in the heart. A thoroughgoing Christian draws his motives of action from his deep heart love for his Master. Up through the roots of his affection for Christ springs an unselfish interest in his brethren. Love imparts to its possessor grace, propriety, and comeliness of deportment. It illuminates the countenance and subdues the voice; it refines and elevates the whole being.

Importance of Little Things

Life is chiefly made up, not of great sacrifices and wonderful achievements, but of little things. It is oftenest through the little things which seem so unworthy of notice that great good or evil is brought into our lives. It is through our failure to endure the tests that come to us in little things, that the habits are molded, the character misshaped; and when the greater tests come, they find us unready. Only by acting upon principle in the tests of daily life can we acquire power to stand firm and faithful in the most dangerous and most difficult positions.

Self-Discipline

We are never alone. Whether we choose Him or not, we have a companion. Remember that wherever you are, whatever you do, God is there. Nothing that is said or done or thought can escape His attention. To your every word or deed you have a witness—the holy, sin-hating God. Before you speak or act, always think of this. As a Christian, you are a member of the royal family, a child of the heavenly King. Say no word, do no act, that shall bring dishonor upon "that worthy name by the which ye are called." James 2:7.

Study carefully the divine-human character, and constantly inquire, "What would Jesus do were He in my place?" This should be the measurement of our duty. Do not place yourselves needlessly in the society of those who by their arts would weaken your purpose to do right, or bring a stain upon your conscience. Do nothing among strangers, in the street, on the cars, in the home, that would have the least appearance of evil. Do something every day to improve, beautify, and ennoble the life that Christ has purchased with His own blood.

Let Principle Guide

Always act from principle, never from impulse. Temper the natural impetuosity of your nature with meekness and gentleness. Indulge in no lightness or trifling. Let no low witticism escape your lips. Even the thoughts are not to be allowed to run riot. They must be restrained, brought into captivity to the obedience of Christ. Let them be placed upon holy things. Then, through the grace of Christ, they will be pure and true.

We need a constant sense of the ennobling power of pure thoughts. The only security for any soul is right thinking. As a man "thinketh in his heart, so is he." Proverbs 23:7. The power of self-restraint strengthens by exercise. That which at first seems difficult, by constant repetition grows easy, until right thoughts and actions become habitual. If we will we may turn away from all that is cheap and inferior, and rise to a high standard; we may be respected by men and beloved of God.

Think and Speak Well of Others

Cultivate the habit of speaking well of others. Dwell upon the good qualities of those with whom you associate, and see as little as possible of their errors and failings. When tempted to complain of what someone has said or done, praise something in that person's life or character. Cultivate thankfulness. Praise God for His wonderful love in giving Christ to die for us. It never pays to think of our grievances. God calls upon us to think of His mercy and His matchless love, that we may be inspired with praise.

Earnest workers have no time for dwelling upon the faults of others. We cannot afford to live on the husks of others' faults or failings. Evilspeaking is a twofold curse, falling more heavily upon the speaker than upon the hearer. He who scatters the seeds of dissension and strife reaps in his own soul the deadly fruits. The very act of looking for evil in others develops evil in those who look. By dwelling upon the faults of others, we are changed into the same image. But by beholding Jesus, talking of His love and perfection of character, we become changed into His image. By contemplating the lofty ideal He has placed before us, we shall be uplifted into a pure and holy atmosphere, even the presence of God. When we abide here, there goes forth from us a light that irradiates all who are connected with us.

Instead of criticizing and condemning others, say, "I must work out my own salvation. If I co-operate with Him who desires to save my soul, I must watch myself diligently. I must put away every evil from my life. I must overcome every fault. I must become a new creature in Christ. Then, instead of weakening those who are striving against evil, I can strengthen them by encouraging words." We are too indifferent in regard to one another. Too often we forget that our fellow laborers are in need of strength and cheer. Take care to assure them of your interest and sympathy. Help them by your prayers, and let them know that you do it.

Patience With the Erring

Not all who profess to be workers for Christ are true disciples. Among those who bear His name, and who are even numbered with His workers, are some who do not represent Him in character. They are not governed by His principles. These persons are often a cause of perplexity and discouragement to their fellow workers who are young in Christian experience; but none need be misled. Christ has given us a perfect example. He bids us follow Him.

Till the end of time there will be tares among the wheat. When the servants of the householder, in their zeal for his honor, asked permission to root out the tares, the master said: "Nay; lest while ye gather up the tares, ye root up also the wheat with them. Let both grow together until the harvest." Matthew 13:29, 30.

In His mercy and long-suffering, God bears patiently with the perverse and even the falsehearted. Among Christ's chosen apostles was Judas the traitor. Should it then be a cause of surprise or discouragement that there are falsehearted ones among His workers today? If He who reads the heart could bear with him who He knew was to be His betrayer, with what patience should we bear with those at fault.

And not all, even of those who appear most faulty, are like Judas. Peter, impetuous, hasty, and self-confident, often appeared to far greater disadvantage than Judas did. He was oftener reproved by the Saviour. But what a life of service and sacrifice was his! What a testimony does it bear to the power of God's grace! So far as we are capable, we are to be to others what Jesus was to His disciples when He walked and talked with them on the earth.

Regard yourselves as missionaries, first of all, among your fellow workers. Often it requires a vast amount of time and labor to win one soul to Christ. And when a soul turns from sin to righteousness, there is joy in the presence of the angels. Think you that the ministering spirits who watch over these souls are pleased to see how indifferently they are treated by some who claim to be Christians? Should Jesus deal with us as we too often deal with one another, who of us could be saved?

Remember that you cannot read hearts. You do not know the motives which prompted the actions that to you look wrong. There are many who have not received a right education; their characters are warped, they are hard and gnarled, and seem to be crooked in every way. But the grace of Christ can transform them. Never cast them aside, never drive them to discouragement or despair by saying, "You have disappointed me, and I will not try to help you." A few words spoken hastily under provocation—just what we think they deserve—may cut the cords of influence that should have bound their hearts to ours.

Influence of a Consistent Christian Life

The consistent life, the patient forbearance, the spirit unruffled under provocation, is always the most conclusive argument and the most solemn appeal. If you have had opportunities and advantages that have not fallen to the lot of others, consider this, and be ever a wise, careful, gentle teacher.

In order to have the wax take a clear, strong impression of the seal, you do not dash the seal upon it in a hasty, violent way; you carefully place the seal on the plastic wax and quietly, steadily press it down until it has hardened in the mold. In like manner deal with human souls. The continuity of Christian influence is the secret of its power, and this depends on the steadfastness of your manifestation of the character of Christ. Help those who have erred, by telling them of your experiences. Show how, when you made grave mistakes, patience, kindness, and helpfulness on the part of your fellow workers gave you courage and hope.

Until the judgment you will never know the influence of a kind, considerate course toward the inconsistent, the unreasonable, the unworthy. When we meet with ingratitude and betrayal of sacred trusts, we are roused to show our contempt or indignation. This the guilty expect; they are prepared for it. But kind forbearance takes them by surprise and often awakens their better impulses and arouses a longing for a nobler life.

"Brethren, if a man be overtaken in a fault, ye which are spiritual, restore such an one in the spirit of meekness; considering thyself, lest thou also be tempted. Bear ye one another's burdens, and so fulfill the law of Christ." Galatians 6:1, 2.

All who profess to be children of God should bear in mind that as missionaries they will be brought into contact with all classes of minds. There are the refined and the coarse, the humble and the proud, the religious and the skeptical, the educated and the ignorant, the rich and the poor. These varied minds cannot be treated alike; yet all need kindness and sympathy. By mutual contact our minds should receive polish and refinement. We are dependent upon one another, closely bound together by the ties of human brotherhood.

> Heaven forming each on other to depend,
> A master or a servant or a friend,
> Bids each on other for assistance call,
> Till one man's weakness grows the strength of all.

It is through the social relations that Christianity comes in contact with the world. Every man or woman who has received the divine illumination is to shed light on the dark pathway of those who are unacquainted with the better way. Social power, sanctified by the Spirit of Christ, must be improved in bringing souls to the Saviour. Christ is not to be hid away in the heart as a coveted treasure, sacred and sweet, to be enjoyed solely by the possessor. We are to have Christ in us as a well of water, springing up into everlasting life, refreshing all who come in contact with us.

Developing Christian Character

Christian life is more than many take it to be. It does not consist wholly in gentleness, patience, meekness, and kindliness. These graces are essential; but there is need also of courage, force, energy, and perseverance. The path that Christ marks out is a narrow, self-denying path. To enter that path and press on through difficulties and discouragements requires men who are more than weaklings.

Force of Character

Men of stamina are wanted, men who will not wait to have their way smoothed and every obstacle removed, men who will inspire with fresh zeal the flagging efforts of dispirited workers, men whose hearts are warm with Christian love and whose hands are strong to do their Master's work.

Some who engage in missionary service are weak,

nerveless, spiritless, easily discouraged. They lack push. They have not those positive traits of character that give power to do something—the spirit and energy that kindle enthusiasm. Those who would win success must be courageous and hopeful. They should cultivate not only the passive but the active virtues. While they are to give the soft answer that turns away wrath, they must possess the courage of a hero to resist evil. With the charity that endures all things, they need the force of character that will make their influence a positive power.

Some have no firmness of character. Their plans and purposes have no definite form and consistency. They are of but little practical use in the world. This weakness, indecision, and inefficiency should be overcome. There is in true Christian character an indomitableness that cannot be molded or subdued by adverse circumstances. We must have moral backbone, an integrity that cannot be flattered, bribed, or terrified.

Mental Culture

God desires us to make use of every opportunity for securing a preparation for His work. He expects us to put all our energies into its performance and to keep our hearts alive to its sacredness and its fearful responsibilities.

Many who are qualified to do excellent work accomplish little because they attempt little. Thousands pass through life as if they had no great object for which to live, no high standard to reach. One reason for this is the low estimate which they place upon themselves. Christ paid an infinite price for us, and according to the price paid He desires us to value ourselves.

Be not satisfied with reaching a low standard. We are not what we might be, or what it is God's will that we should be. God has given us reasoning powers, not to remain inactive, or to be perverted to earthly and sordid pursuits, but that they may be developed to the utmost, refined, sanctified, ennobled, and used in advancing the interests of His kingdom.

None should consent to be mere machines, run by another man's mind. God has given us ability, to think and to act, and it is by acting with carefulness, looking to Him for wisdom that you will become capable of bearing burdens. Stand in your God-given personality. Be no other person's shadow. Expect that the Lord will work in and by and through you.

Never think that you have learned enough, and that you may now relax your efforts. The cultivated mind is the measure of the man. Your education should continue during your lifetime; every day you should be learning and putting to practical use the knowledge gained.

Remember that in whatever position you may serve you are revealing motive, developing character. Whatever your work, do it with exactness, with diligence; overcome the inclination to seek an easy task.

How Do You Work?

The same spirit and principles that one brings into the daily labor will be brought into the whole life. Those who desire a fixed amount to do and a fixed salary, and who wish to prove an exact fit without the trouble of adaptation or training, are not the ones whom God calls to work in His cause. Those who study how to give as little as possible of their physical, mental, and moral power are not the workers upon whom He can pour out abundant blessings. Their example is contagious. Self-interest is the ruling motive. Those who need to be watched and who work only as every duty is specified to them, are not the ones who will be pronounced good and faithful. Workers are needed who manifest energy, integrity, diligence, those who are willing to do anything that needs to be done.

Many become inefficient by evading responsibilities for fear of failure. Thus they fail of gaining that education which results from experience, and which reading and study and all the advantages otherwise gained cannot give them.

Man can shape circumstances, but circumstances should not be allowed to shape the man. We should seize upon circumstances as instruments by which to work. We are to master them, but should not permit them to master us.

Men of power are those who have been opposed,

baffled, and thwarted. By calling their energies into action, the obstacles they meet prove to them positive blessings. They gain self-reliance. Conflict and perplexity call for the exercise of trust in God and for that firmness which develops power.

The Motive in Service

Christ gave no stinted service. He did not measure His work by hours. His time, His heart, His soul and strength, were given to labor for the benefit of humanity. Through weary days He toiled, and through long nights He bent in prayer for grace and endurance that He might do a larger work. With strong crying and tears He sent His petitions to heaven, that His human nature might be strengthened, that He might be braced to meet the wily foe in all his deceptive workings, and fortified to fulfill His missions of uplifting humanity. To His workers He says, "I have given you an example, that ye should do as I have done." John 13:15.

"The love of Christ," said Paul, "constraineth us." 2 Corinthians 5:14. This was the actuating principle of his conduct; it was his motive power. If ever his ardor in the path of duty flagged for a moment, one glance at the Cross caused him to gird up anew the loins of his mind and press forward in the way of self-denial. In his labors for his brethren he relied much upon the manifestation of infinite love in the sacrifice of Christ, with its subduing, constraining power.

How earnest, how touching, his appeal: "Ye know the grace of our Lord Jesus Christ, that, though He was rich, yet for your sakes He became poor, that ye through His poverty might be rich." 2 Corinthians 8:9. You know the height from which He stooped, the depth of humiliation to which He descended. His feet entered upon the path of sacrifice and turned not aside until He had given His life. There was no rest for Him between the throne in heaven and the Cross. His love for man led Him to welcome every indignity and suffer every abuse.

Paul admonishes us to "look not every man on his own things, but every man also on the things of others." He bids us possess the mind "which was also in Christ Jesus: who, being in the form of God, thought it not robbery to be equal with God: but made Himself of no reputation, and took upon Him the form of a servant, and was made in the likeness of men: and being found in fashion as a man, He humbled Himself, and became obedient unto death, even the death of the cross." Philippians 2:4-8.

Paul was deeply anxious that the humiliation of Christ should be seen and realized. He was convinced that if men could be led to consider the amazing sacrifice made by the Majesty of heaven, selfishness would be banished from their hearts. The apostle lingers over point after point, that we may in some measure comprehend the wonderful condescension of the Saviour in behalf of sinners. He directs the mind first to the position which Christ occupied in heaven in the bosom of His Father; he reveals Him afterward as laying aside His glory, voluntarily subjecting Himself to the humbling conditions of man's life, assuming the responsibilities of a servant, and becoming obedient unto death, and that the most ignominious and revolting, the most agonizing—the death of the cross. Can we contemplate this wonderful manifestation of the love of God without gratitude and love, and a deep sense of the fact that we are not our own? Such a Master should not be served from grudging, selfish motives.

"Ye know," says Peter, "that ye were not redeemed with corruptible things, as silver and gold." 1 Peter 1:18. Oh, had these been sufficient to purchase the salvation of man, how easily it might have been accomplished by Him who says, "The silver is Mine, and the gold is Mine"! Haggai 2:8. But the sinner could be redeemed only by the precious blood of the Son of God. Those who, failing to appreciate this wonderful sacrifice, withhold themselves from Christ's service, will perish in their selfishness.

Singleness of Purpose

In the life of Christ, everything was made subordinate to His work, the great work of redemption which He came to accomplish. And the same devotion, the same self-denial and sacrifice, the same subjection to the claims of the Word of God, is to be manifest in His disciples.

Everyone who accepts Christ as his personal Saviour will long for the privilege of serving God. Contemplating what heaven has done for him, his heart is moved with boundless love and adoring gratitude. He is eager to signalize his gratitude by devoting his abilities to God's service. He longs to show his love for Christ and for His purchased possession. He covets toil, hardship, sacrifice.

The true worker for God will do his best, because in so doing he can glorify his Master. He will do right in order to regard the requirements of God. He will endeavor to improve all his faculties. He will perform every duty as unto God. His one desire will be that Christ may receive homage and perfect service.

There is a picture representing a bullock standing between a plow and an altar, with the inscription, "Ready for either," ready to toil in the furrow or to be offered on the altar of sacrifice. This is the position of the true child of God—willing to go where duty calls, to deny self, to sacrifice for the Redeemer's cause.

Pressing Toward the Mark

We need constantly a fresh revelation of Christ, a daily experience that harmonizes with His teachings. High and holy attainments are within our reach. Continual progress in knowledge and virtue is God's purpose for us. His law is the echo of His own voice, giving to all the invitation, "Come up higher. Be holy, holier still." Every day we may advance in perfection of Christian character.

Those who are engaged in service for the Master need an experience much higher, deeper, broader, than many have yet thought of having. Many who are already members of God's great family know little of what it means to behold His glory and to be changed from glory to glory. Many have a twilight perception of Christ's excellence, and their hearts thrill with joy. They long for a fuller, deeper sense of the Saviour's love. Let these cherish every desire of the soul after God.

The Holy Spirit works with those who will be worked, molds those who will be molded, fashions those who will be fashioned. Give yourselves the culture of spiritual thoughts and holy communings. You have seen but the first rays of the early dawn of His glory. As you follow on to know the Lord, you will know that "the path of the righteous is as the light of dawn, that shineth more and more unto the perfect day." Proverbs 4:18, R.V., margin.

The Joy of the Lord

"These things have I spoken unto you," said Christ, "that My joy might remain in you, and that your joy might be full." John 15:11.

Ever before Him, Christ saw the result of His mission. His earthly life, so full of toil and self-sacrifice, was cheered by the thought that He would not have all this travail for nought. By giving His life for the life of men, He would restore in humanity the image of God. He would lift us up from the dust, reshape the character after the pattern of His own character, and make it beautiful with His own glory.

Christ saw of the travail of His soul and was satisfied. He viewed the expanse of eternity and saw the happiness of those who through His humiliation should receive pardon and everlasting life. He was wounded for their transgressions, bruised for their iniquities. The chastisement of their peace was upon Him, and with

His stripes they were healed. He heard the shout of the redeemed. He heard the ransomed ones singing the song of Moses and the Lamb. Although the baptism of blood must first be received, although the sins of the world were to weigh upon His innocent soul, although the shadow of an unspeakable woe was upon Him; yet for the joy that was set before Him He chose to endure the cross and despised the shame.

This joy all His followers are to share. However great and glorious hereafter, our reward is not all to be reserved for the time of final deliverance. Even here we are by faith to enter into the Saviour's joy. Like Moses, we are to endure as seeing the Invisible.

Now the church is militant. Now we are confronted with a world in darkness, almost wholly given over to idolatry. But the day is coming when the battle will have been fought, the victory won. The will of God is to be done on earth as it is done in heaven. The nations of the saved will know no other law than the law of heaven. All will be a happy, united family, clothed with the garments of praise and thanksgiving—the robe of Christ's righteousness. All nature, in its surpassing loveliness, will offer to God a tribute of praise and adoration. The world will be bathed in the light of heaven. The light of the moon will be as the light of the sun, and the light of the sun will be sevenfold greater than it is now. The years will move on in gladness. Over the scene the morning stars will sing together, the sons of

God will shout for joy, while God and Christ will unite in proclaiming, "There shall be no more sin, neither shall there be any more death."

These visions of future glory, scenes pictured by the hand of God, should be dear to His children.

Evaluating the Things of Time and Eternity

Stand on the threshold of eternity and hear the gracious welcome given to those who in this life have co-operated with Christ, regarding it as a privilege and an honor to suffer for His sake. With the angels, they cast their crowns at the feet of the Redeemer, exclaiming, "Worthy is the Lamb that was slain to receive power, and riches, and wisdom, and strength, and honor, and glory, and blessing. . . . Honor, and glory, and power, be unto Him that sitteth upon the throne, and unto the Lamb for ever and ever." Revelation 5:12, 13.

There the redeemed ones greet those who directed them to the uplifted Saviour. They unite in praising Him who died that human beings might have the life that measures with the life of God. The conflict is over. All tribulation and strife are at an end. Songs of victory fill all heaven, as the redeemed stand around the throne of God. All take up the joyful strain, "Worthy is the Lamb that was slain" and hath redeemed us to God.

"I beheld, and, lo, a great multitude, which no man could number, of all nations, and kindreds, and people, and tongues, stood before the throne, and before the Lamb, clothed with white robes, and palms in their hands; and cried with a loud voice, saying, Salvation to our God which sitteth upon the throne, and unto the Lamb." Revelation 7:9, 10.

"These are they which came out of great tribulation, and have washed their robes, and made them white in the blood of the Lamb. Therefore are they before the throne of God, and serve Him day and night in His temple: and He that sitteth on the throne shall dwell among them. They shall hunger no more, neither thirst any more; neither shall the sun light on them, nor any heat. For the Lamb which is in the midst of the throne shall feed them, and shall lead them unto living fountains of waters: and God shall wipe away all tears from their eyes.

"And there shall be no more death, neither sorrow, nor crying, neither shall there be any more pain: for the former things are passed away." Verses 14-17; 21:4.

We need to keep ever before us this vision of things unseen. It is thus that we shall be able to set a right value on the things of eternity and the things of time. It is this that will give us power to influence others for the higher life.

In the Mount With God

"Come up to Me into the mount," God bids us. To Moses, before he could be God's instrument in delivering Israel, was appointed the forty years of communion with Him in the mountain solitudes. Before bearing God's message to Pharaoh, he spoke with the angel in the burning bush. Before receiving God's law as the representative of His people, he was called into the mount, and beheld His glory. Before executing justice on the idolaters, he was hidden in the cleft of the rock, and the Lord said, "I will proclaim the name of the Lord before thee," "merciful and gracious, slow to anger, and abundant in loving-kindness and truth; . . . and that will by no means clear the guilty." Exodus 33:19; 34:6, 7, A.R.V. Before he laid down, with his life, his burden for Israel, God called him to the top of Pisgah and spread out before him the glory of the Promised Land.

Before the disciples went forth on their mission, they were called up into the mount with Jesus. Before the power and glory of Pentecost, came the night of communion with the Saviour, the meeting on the mountain in Galilee, the parting scene upon Olivet, with the angel's promise, and the days of prayer and communion in the upper chamber.

Jesus, when preparing for some great trial or some important work, would resort to the solitude of the mountains and spend the night in prayer to His Father. A night of prayer preceded the ordination of the apostles and the Sermon on the Mount, the Transfiguration, the agony of the judgment hall and the Cross, and the Resurrection glory.

Communion With God in Prayer

We, too, must have times set apart for meditation and prayer and for receiving spiritual refreshing. We do not value the power and efficacy of prayer as we should. Prayer and faith will do what no power on earth can accomplish. We are seldom, in all respects, placed in the same position twice. We continually have new scenes and new trials to pass through, where past experience cannot be a sufficient guide. We must have the continual light that comes from God.

Christ is ever sending messages to those who listen for His voice. On the night of the agony in Gethsemane, the sleeping disciples heard not the voice of Jesus. They had a dim sense of the angels' presence, but lost the power and glory of the scene. Because of their drowsiness and stupor they failed of receiving the evidence that would have strengthened their souls for the terrible scenes before them. Thus today the very men who most need divine instruction often fail of receiving it, because they do not place themselves in communion with heaven.

The temptations to which we are daily exposed make prayer a necessity. Dangers beset every path. Those who are seeking to rescue others from vice and ruin are especially exposed to temptation. In constant contact with evil, they need a strong hold upon God lest they themselves be corrupted. Short and decisive are the

steps that lead men down from high and holy ground to a low level. In a moment decisions may be made that fix one's condition forever. One failure to overcome leaves the soul unguarded. One evil habit, if not firmly resisted, will strengthen into chains of steel, binding the whole man.

The reason why so many are left to themselves in places of temptation is that they do not set the Lord always before them. When we permit our communion with God to be broken, our defense is departed from us. Not all your good purposes and good intentions will enable you to withstand evil. You must be men and women of prayer. Your petitions must not be faint, occasional, and fitful, but earnest, persevering, and constant. It is not always necessary to bow upon your knees in order to pray. Cultivate the habit of talking with the Saviour when you are alone, when you are walking, and when you are busy with your daily labor. Let the heart be continually uplifted in silent petition for help, for light, for strength, for knowledge. Let every breath be a prayer.

As workers for God we must reach men where they are, surrounded with darkness, sunken in vice, and stained with corruption. But while we stay our minds upon Him who is our sun and our shield, the evil that surrounds us will not bring one stain upon our garments. As we work to save the souls that are ready to perish we shall not be put to shame if we make God our trust. Christ in the heart, Christ in the life, this is our safety. The atmosphere of His presence will fill the soul with abhorrence of all that is evil. Our spirit may be so identified with His that in thought and aim we shall be one with Him.

It was through faith and prayer that Jacob, from being a man of feebleness and sin, became a prince with God. It is thus that you may become men and women of high and holy purpose, of noble life, men and women who will not for any consideration be swayed from truth, right, and justice. All are pressed with urgent cares, burdens, and duties, but the more difficult your position and the heavier your burdens, the more you need Jesus.

It is a serious mistake to neglect the public worship of God. The privileges of divine service should not be lightly regarded. Those who attend upon the sick are often unable to avail themselves of these privileges, but they should be careful not to absent themselves needlessly from the house of worship.

In ministering to the sick, more than in any merely secular business, success depends on the spirit of consecration and self-sacrifice with which the work is done. Those who bear responsibilities need to place themselves where they will be deeply impressed by the Spirit of God. You should have as much greater anxiety than do others for the aid of the Holy Spirit and for a knowledge of God as your position of trust is more responsible than that of others.

Nothing is more needed in our work than the practical results of communion with God. We should show by our daily lives that we have peace and rest in the Saviour. His peace in the heart will shine forth in the countenance. It will give to the voice a persuasive power. Communion with God will ennoble the character and the life. Men will take knowledge of us, as of the first disciples, that we have been with Jesus. This will impart to the worker a power that nothing else can give. Of this power he must not allow himself to be deprived.

We must live a twofold life—a life of thought and action, of silent prayer and earnest work. The strength received through communion with God, united with earnest effort in training the mind to thoughtfulness and caretaking, prepares one for daily duties and keeps the spirit in peace under all circumstances, however trying.

The Divine Counselor

When in trouble, many think they must appeal to some earthly friend, telling him their perplexities, and begging for help. Under trying circumstances unbelief fills their hearts, and the way seems dark. And all the time there stands beside them the mighty Counselor of the ages, inviting them to place their confidence in Him. Jesus, the great Burden Bearer, is saying, "Come unto Me, and I will give you rest." Shall we turn from Him to uncertain human beings, who are as dependent upon God as we ourselves are?